Windmills in …

TOM RAWORTH was born in Lond… published more than forty books and p… translations. His graphic work has b… …pe, the United States and South Africa, and h… …n readings of his poems worldwide: most recently in China and Mexico. In 2007 in Italy he was awarded the Antonio Delfini Prize for Lifetime Achievement – although he is not yet dead, but living in Brighton.

Also by Tom Raworth from Carcanet Press

Collected Poems

TOM RAWORTH

Windmills in Flames

Old and New Poems

CARCANET

First published in Great Britain in 2010 by

Carcanet Press Limited
Alliance House
Cross Street
Manchester M2 7AQ

A CIP catalogue record for this book is available from the British Library

ISBN 978 1 84777 082 0

The publisher acknowledges financial assistance from Arts Council England

Typeset by XL Publishing Services, Tiverton
Printed and bound in England by SRP Ltd, Exeter

…small wars are operations undertaken under executive authority, wherein military force is combined with diplomatic pressure in the internal or external affairs of another state whose government is unstable, inadequate, or unsatisfactory for the preservation of life and of such interests as are determined by the foreign policy of our Nation.

United States Marine Corps, *Small Wars Manual*

"Flowers in their wounds," muttered the airman, "that's what she couldn't get over, flowers in their wounds, flowers."

Barbara Euphan Todd, *Miss Ranskill Comes Home*

This book is for Hannah, Belinda,
Victoria and Ruth, with gratitude and love.

Acknowledgements

Some of these poems were first published in *Bad Press*; *Blue Pig*; *Buffalo News*; *Counterpunch*; *Critical Quarterly*; *Desperate for Love*; *Dusie 6*; *Ecopoetics*; *Invisible Tight Institutional Outer Flanks Dub (verb) Glorious National Hi-Violence Response Dream*; *Lifecoach*; *Matter*; *Past Simple*; *Square One*; *Starting at Zero*; *The i.e. Reader*; *Tits* and *Zoland Poetry*; also as a limited edition of twenty copies handmade for the First Pearl River Poetry Conference, Guangzhou, China, June 2005; and in comic-book form as a series of twenty-nine prints.

In the USA poems were first published in the books *Pleasant Butter* (Sand Project Press, Northampton, MA, and Paris, France, editors/publishers David Ball and George Tysh); *Caller* (Edge Books, Washington DC, editor/publisher Rod Smith), *Let Baby Fall* (Critical Documents, Providence RI, editor/publisher Justin Katko) and *Tottering State* (O Books, Berkeley, CA, editor/publisher Lesley Scalapino). I thank everyone involved with those publications.

The first thirteen poems included here were omitted from *Collected Poems* (Carcanet, 2003). 'Cap' (*Act*, Trigram Press, 1973) was missing because of the author's carelessness; 'Into the Wild Blue Yonder', 'Breeding the Arsenic-Proof Baby' (*Tottering State*, O Books, 2000) and the ten poems following (*Pleasant Butter*, Sand Project Press, 1972) because copies of the original publications could not be found at that time.

Thanks to Pierre Joris for recovering 'Intellectual Compost 6', written on the flyleaf of his copy of *Collected Poems*.

'With John Gian' is a collaboration written for *Markers* at the Peggy Guggenheim Collection, Venice Biennale, 2001.

'Listen Up' was written to infiltrate the 'Poets for the War' website and submitted under the name Ophelia Merkin. It was sufficiently successful for Ophelia to be invited to take over the site before Robert Creeley blew her cover.

'Data Death : Zerone' was recited by Rudy Giuliani. G.W. Bush plagiarised 'Shuck' in a video-conference during the battle of Fallujah.

Contents

Into the Wild Blue Yonder

prisoners
christmas

our
ower

pour
power

"43" he said, referring to the numbers they'd given the
background noise tapes

Cap

pattern outside my head
speak to me
signaller of the word-commune

i was not aware
one lonely word outside
could call itself 'snap'

Breeding the Arsenic-Proof Baby

i see china as terribly peaceful folk
sitting around saying "torch-singer roxy's
on the wire" writing poems like

'24 ribs

pop out flies the spirit'

i like to listen late at night
breathing in a tiny cloud of chinese skin
as they all jump up and down whispering "china"

they give it away
with pleasant butter

★

T H I N K

★

we rise to the top of the stairs
before a harp's shadow

they are playing play
d/c to a/c

who
cares

★

'my' cheek itches
'i' scratch 'it' with 'my' forefinger

★

prompted by the next world

★

i thought is a
mirror i
thought

random is one of the laws
one of which is recognising it

In the Beginning Was the Word, and the Word Was With God, and the Word Was God

form of the word
is heated
and dropped on mind

the shape it burns
depends upon
memory and imagination

a perfect mix
of their solutions
is totally inflammable

so all is revealed
or we are
branded

Rather a Few Mistakes than Fucking Boredom

giant cameras whirring
on the lens hood of each
stands a rifleman

his warning shot
as the image approaches
sounds in the past

today we are scraping
every particle from the tin
cocoa-tin telephones

smell of steam trains
unable to act his deformity
sounds every where

empty affects all thinking
whistling sounds
as the familiar voice sells its pretension

(oh guide my hand
to make these tracks
i do not understand

soft needle mind
now fills all grooves
to amplify time's wind)

Art is the Farthest Retreat from Boredom

every thing is replacing
the inside of being there

'the true aristocrat
of the equestrian world'

death is so obvious
what does not exist is eternity

any thing can do nothing *but*
prove it because we are now

Preserved People are Rare

we are not here for a test
dance every one dance

who's collecting the midgets?
my reflexes are so slow

curious is a direction
why permutate the bits

to find now? you are
all bits other wise

the end

Ground Swell

out in the fresh air
captain phillips hadn't told her
she gave him two helpings of larks

beginning
middle
end

Drop in Existence

i am lonely for my replaced cells
1945, 1952, 1959, 1966, 1973, 1980, 1987

learn your language
no direction *is* home

Vague

silver moon
in a red world

running all day
rattling through dry forest

pleasant butter
is silver and gold

never used up my energy
burned out the connections

i’ve got
to know

Thor Heyerdahl Solved the Mystery of the Statues? That *Wasn't the Mystery*

true sight of the enemy
is not you

noble journeys
into the unmapped

i mean the boredom
of a kon-tiki

against leif ericsson
courage and knowledge

are not enough
pleasant butter again

How to Patronise a Poem

begin
welcome in

appear
poem
in these lines

i will
not draw
your picture

★

no. the spark comes. we work together. oh it is form, form, the making of distinctions. form, the shape revealed by the detection, in all dimensions, of the boundaries of content

★

stunting their *own* growth... making *themselves* ornamental japanese trees, safe, instead of being the *trees struck by lightning*

★

'extra yields
extra profits'

as if what they handle
were not alive

★

life was the invader, perhaps, and all things that live were members of the crew (animals went in two by two, yin and yang) who survived through a warp into no-space between

★

i sense the end
down a tube
a spurt now and then

eighteenth to eighteenth
a choice
of the net's size and gauge

the ship is changing course
i have played out the games
and the old faces bore me

season to season
names flashing
i'll hammer it

so damn thin
i can see out

*

our enquiry
points a way
off the wheel

eleven segments
are left to trust
and imagination

*

lose
your   self

your   self
     becomes
your   art

then what is left

lives

no matter how you muddy it

it clears
and there you are

again

★

do you see me?
i am leaving a space
where i was   is as bad

★

i shall forge the blade
of my own substance

and it may not be a blade

★

i have tasted fire
goodbye, pleasant butter

Intellectual Compost 6

clusters from a level best
company remain under accuracy
for minutes of last revenue
detach and screw you

good people in box pieces
absorb basic lies
gingerly rattle tall cottons
hung still on the front page

snickering worked great pictures
sapped traction for spectators
face up arms pointed out
broke apart stunted emotions

nothing could deprive conversion
of fire shared to appreciate despair
nothing reflective but movie love
touched costume almost evaporated

Consolidation

so large attending to increase
clambered desperately into some air
would surely frighten weekend excursions

you could pay players
an introverted interest
ask them to rip frequency

examined every one real
becomes the forum on sight
spasmodic leaps in a foreign room

look hideous awash with opinions
followed by dissociation shown protruding
discovered money business

transmuted through the subject metal
guaranteeing more dramatic things
phrase donkey work settled back

open the last door inside
close to wind and modern air
build up a local anaesthetic

begging not to be beaten
themselves in their consumption
but for the notary's mind drift

through rains southward across officialdom
we know the alligators
who circulate around thinking

to assess the human angle
oldest surviving peeling walls
exorbitant doubts almost organised

show people supporting scaffolding
fastidious views too
demonstrate the perception of statement

Systems Disruption

flags every utility silence filtered
what would blossom to conclude form from
skin accidentally imported during influence
done parade reforming footage reduced
normally sit round problems
authority plays two tunes in season

filtered what imported plays from skin
would conclude sit parade flags tunes
influence done to two in round
accidentally during footage every
sea blossom reduced normally problems
authority silence reforming form utility

26

affects more than four million
for the president's decision wi
specialist in diagnosing cere
then moving to a nursing home fr
of his confusions he spoke of th
doctors he had known at harvard
to develop an idea he didn't seem
on grand rounds at boston city h
a point that he was making even t
1912 he speaks about his grade-s
know that at these moments he be
he did not appear to know at firs
in a congenial voice as if the tw
a patient suddenly collapsed mo
in the practiced way that docto
about to leave his room he took m
yiddish still he thought for a m
when i visit now i try to take my d
tail and sits in front of him and
reach his hand to stroke her hea
lost that skill so how's it been p
i was there did you get it all don
he'll simply press my arm and hol
his recognition of my face is no
the grave financial worries th
allow my mother who is 96 y

for Bruce Ackley

Translation 2

amour-qui-essai in called god merciful
mine muselmanischen the siblings in the chaste earth of pakistan
the civilians and the soldiers, the peace and gottbenediktionen are on you.
crusade against the intensified islam and the slaughter of the antennas of muhammad
put in boxes the peace of god
and benediktionen increased là-dessus for being a lot in afghanistan.

the world has been divided in two stocks:
under the pointer of the crossing the president george w of the united states
infidelitykopf of bushes as an example
and the other under the pointer of the islam appreciated

the government of pakistan is under the pointer of the satisfied crossing.
expected all the powerful god: from the hypokriten the happy tidings of elasticity
then the damage for they; but one hard punishment;
yea to those that they take for unbelievers rather like freundbelievers:
is it an honour that they search between them?
nay the entire honour is with god. defending of or the islam
it is your day, in order to carry the islam.

that one, that it believes to god and doomsday
can not be rested to comfort,
until that it recognises well
and to its defenders and to.

Spime

emotion searchlight
yellow flat

mini war
more focus

delivery
of advanced

network technology
to europe

panama hats
spin over the continent

With John Gian

putting a hand through concrete
figures ahead turned into space

polychrome signs dilate time
in wavelets of colour-shifting sand

fish gleam in love with pragmatics
but blankets seem to be asleep

space ripples between words
fixed to an old idea

admit you are the narrator
tempted to look at brain holes

let flow without pause
sonorous ambience of birds and violins

absolutely contagious for used blues
attitude commands the state

a circular squared route
predominantly green at its centre

events know our levels
extremes are cheaper than excess

the hand reveals depth
arm entangled in the lament

fight for balance along silhouettes
faded navy blue focus in the glare

a steady pace slightly spread-legged
a strong almost invisible presence

perhaps a sticking long time
gestures between two of them

something not quite filters through eyelashes
an unlikely game at such long distance

Caller

last century
pose half
deep bass in which
unknowing

con moto
with sloppy surface
percussion apart

mentions
regular welcoming
prepared to go
sucked

whereas maudlin
oppression sears
table trends
report

about our movies
out and beyond
partying herd

period confession
on drums and signed
word has it

define
clarity chosen interplay
provide
pull

mushrooms wet with dew
between two lions
empty shape

creator of spartacus
vectored with released pause

chicken with rice
but here
get through
aftermath of glass

on what could
risk suffocation
embarrassing death

one hand wriggled through
metal visited his nostrils

lights were on
closed on
to speed at a distance
present

favourite nightmares
transposed
move recently ballet

brutality
not yet completed
hot-wired control

perpetual smoke closed doors
never impede
species

monitored
by authorities
half a mile shaking

limousines full of heads
cheap disposability

age of exponentials
kurdish women
carry brush

mere human beings
faster than that
nervous system

who look for guidance
as reflection of ritual

exactly
assumed larksong
forgot blood suppression

knowing it will pass
shouldn't stop you
helping it go

interfere with nature
mary
o lanza liar

vada vaguer
vitalities
cloudy
underworld

some testing requires
software called
'it prevailed' to print

suffer together
down logic
and intuition

target parasite life
fused to its surface
with drugs

that an awestruck
vegetable
of the temperate zone

wore off
bewildered
within moments he recognised

devastated repeating character
prefers jeans

dazzling morning lies
sparkling thinking dust
motes
dance wrong

cancers dictate detection
to search out every gene

repressed when awake
rely
on their own conclusion

tiny through
particular meaning
mysterious

strength
can depopulate
blades adapted
quiet movement

plastic half-light
increase production
oil and water

victories opened deep
operating light values

partisan widespread belief
speculate in sound waves

anathema
mostly a string
glowed in the half dark

lesser branches
captured grow suspicious
informal

fashions in eating
based on shape
one two three four five

there's only one of you
mere sight of kind nomadic

cue there goes god
set them shone
meaning few in their suites

fire of thought
why work for afraid
rather than angry

human decoration
resisted in every way

not the general good
round deaths up or down
to tidy

the best for each other
next year in jerusalem

don't mind us
go on with your war
we're for lost city

odd mint sun
you towing harrow
rectify root slew

understanding
what intuition
writes in language

all of the yellow stuff
was coming out of the ground

at dawn
against blurred colours
on my closed eyelids
dance

bent wisteria
the friendly shadows
of the dead

iris flames
taste of dry stone
born to detect nothing

clay brown stuff you
are doing something with
and burn it

sweet silhouettes look forward
there will be a garden

alleviate directed up
on siren fashion

offering
antiphoton even
to those composed

observe
flip tunnel noise
introduction
not rising

dying itches
imploding light
space stationary

this train is
dimensionally
very delicate

no to aitch pit
nah the soot even
coats their rapture

'the scourge of gay marriage
upgrades this category'

traces
dotted cotton strip
after capture with heads

officers gape
although emerging
devoted sense

personal actions
cannot fix nor
prevent fruitcake

at bottom disease
dealt
with strategic explosions

light traffic
aimed at brains
brought hot food
to mouth with fork

death seen in frame spin in cave
bird in box in brook line

divest intended
purchasing it in
profession

log on automatically
herself
engraves troubles

all greens
a spark of human cost
those went so strangely

memory reshuffling
toned mortar
play in coiled dark

in shadow shadows
media cycle manicures

cream flakes
from leaden cows
hits wear formal horizons

toward prior to delivery
citation's absurd

borrowed complete shock
extend instructional assist

sleepers open
state of siege
rebels tended to frown

menace without epiphanies
malice placid reach

have tenth reservoirs
cutback tax cuts
not shared sharply

condition paused
above space
of unknown provenance

adequate strudels
separately dressed
affect marble

tripwire recalls
mist tinged orange
from left wall to right

a marketed skillet
blitzed stocking
cat on diesel

full print to work
perfume preposterous name
nuisance

velveeta cheese modelled
clings to guide
as per quartet

restripe the lot
emphases became effective fund

dwindle animate slides
torqued into gouge designs bone

entrepreneurial tunnel
dash tricks right
fitted

head too funny
turned endless cordite
tattoo lightning

ideological rules
mandate measure
mistakes

clog robot
bladder waves discharge
a distilled spinach

paramilitary wreckage
arks one musical

fierce turn crucial
shift forgiveness
you jolt that table

nature corrupt nature
romped bound constituency

non-electrical devil
is this thought
calculus

all were buxom
mushroom and oyster
interested

knows knots
future wardrobes
pin to scratch
on underneath

provide physical support
sweeping public spaces

samples ideally
equal random chance
wildly cough

water stained
site of passion
on the front
of these books

oozed pink layers
small slide for five
iodine poultice

balancing as a hawk
drawn downward
failing judgment

thoughts open gateway
long enough to believe
posture

extremes of those
retreating
indication objects

space has background
light area in traditional

invented colour
beaming from tunnel
closed in film

ambient paddock
sheets blue glass
equilibrium

as two rival identities
backwards in red shirts

boast cast off
celebration
to map
disabled lines

to understand thought
be no explicable reason

appropriate health
eliminates from image
change

questions gathering
internal
rough rhythms invoke

defence of culture
narrator intervenes
headache

game of blue
shadow you shall rise
high in the city

merely mammals
strung her to the willow
cross the way

peru diseuse
sonic hedgehog spectrum
mighty low

holoprosencephaly
east lack
bruise become bone

abandoned
property
a dangerous animal

even a regulated
public utility

ant smuggling
insufficient windows
a crusty boat

"hitler come on
i'll buy you
a glass of lemonade"

in concrete block pens
of an idle hog growing barn

fid def ind imp
nicaragua
i was ready

for a new
spoon river
anthology of real dead

pickups in sepia
desert air
up with the sun

fine structure
constant
stone spectre he is
a deep pig

burnt lily
tracking workers
lawyers describe organs

in the luxury
of our poverty
is the choice

to switch
from choral evensong
to andy kershaw

one point perspective path
to what is not remembered

lightning trammel
camion and kratos
stop and search

egalitarian
segmental
acephalous

monotony of renewal
with no sense of smell

their woes otherwise
impact he emphatic
immune

recorded underwater suspect
deformed from sphere

grilled details flashing
fatally pursued
across glass

slow de
light print organ
skin ne
compte plus pour du beur

when part be assembled
possible camera completes

Envoi

I could go on like this all day
Ti-tum ti-tum and doodly-ay
With every now and then a glance
To see if I've still on my pants
And if I have, if that stain's jism
Or just a trace of modernism.

For isn't this what poetry is?...
A raincoat over similes
You've seen before... FLASH...look again
The same. No need to strain your brain
Simply recline on the chaise longue
And listen to the rhymes go bong.

And on like this ad infinitum
With a metrical change or two to brighten
The gloomy rhythm of these stanzas
(Metaphor a Belgium for my Panzers).
Let those who think that piss is water
Sup deeply this insipid Porter.

Listen Up

Why should we listen to Hans Blix
and all those other foreign pricks:
the faggot French who swallow snails
and kiss the cheeks of other males:
the Germans with their Nazi past
and leather pants and cars that last
longer than ours: the ungrateful Chinks
we let make all our clothes; those finks
should back us in whatever task –
we shouldn't even have to ask:
and as for creepy munchkin Putin...
a slimy asshole – no disputing!?
We saved those Russians from the reds –
they owe support. Those wimpish heads
of tiny states without the power
to have a radio in the shower
should fall in line behind George Bush
and join with him and Blair to push
the sword of truth through Saddam's guts
(no need for any ifs or buts)
we'll even do it without the backing
of UN cowards and their quacking –
remember how we thrashed the Nips
and fried them like potato chips?
God's on our side, he's white and Yankee
he'd drop the bombs, he'd drive a tank: we
know he's stronger than their Allah
as is our righteousness and valor!
We'll clip Mohammed's ears and pecker
And then move on to napalm Mecca.

Coda to a Laureate

If I could take my tongue out of your arse
(Though drag me as a train down aisles you tread)
The tiny Royal turd upon my tongue
Would quiver as my heart that you are wed.

Seesound

cutting paste

one out
can only grow if different
tiles muted though not
biographies
mean of impression
means of expression
will sing
enough times steamed
turn volume up
to swamp static
even the veil
has gradations of tone
focus has come to conclusion

from surface

relax into gravity
sun's rival
nerve out
rest your eyes
before starvation
no room for present
dread in a book
sufficient
to keep heat off
added value water

half light

delays into gravity

no room for poignant
no room for pregnant

added while water
added whole water

Issue them Gasmasks

acanth ad aest
chel coen bi
dactyl ect haem
kino labi

pter pneu sarc
scaph peri erythr
zo vita ultra
macro nephr

for Bill Fuller

Language Construction

for Doug Lang

Equitable Deviation

there is no definitive answer
no licence can assure
to a culture of their own
the enlivening element
breathing room pressure
when diverse unavowed purposes
purse and politics for the murderers
involve an erroneous standard
primary chaos repairing a marketing point
of actual not deemed death
influence pledges to abide
feeding and hydration courtesy of mars
cultivating that corner of wilderness
child and putative father

a ration of melted sheep
the seedbearing bugalu
rarely gives up storage mechanisms
invokes in terrorem
planted by a christmas basket
soberly enticing heirs
a spin cycle of glum capers
to reap their fill
between direct sounds blurs
with diamond-like clarity
the image elimination game-show
exactly seven pigeons
before black becomes a safe place
greet them when they arrive

(Tom Raworth and William Fuller)

Baggage Claim
(a slugging welterweight natural)

monitors will certainly appreciate
my soles are vibram
swung to keep low profile
hubris in one act
each an evacuation slide
supple mental flotation
may be behind you
tighter straps
a life attendant
of a global lifespan
technological dildoes accurately shot
straight off what was left
between idealism and hope
create interest in card readers
rationale beyond acquisition
a lacy white statue parched
bronze beneath shit on a stick
when colour disappeared

inflexible in acknowledgment
of doubt

much too now deals with war
bamboo screech on various types
physical technical amusing animation
without leave there is no colour
approximately to slow fire
washers without leave
or cold spray with vinegar
a football field of silence
under the helicopter
boutgates and ambages
running around water
slow discs of fire
physical technology amuses
bamboo presses boring cries
without vacation

at the cold throw
jealous mothers of light
transregeneration

in evening of black and white
become they

grubs in burgundy
none were injured in making
by the screen
the way it is hung
shorter ones
hardy with good air
falling through glass
if they believe that
they'll believe anything
this whole energy factor
nicknamed the biscuit
on wings of a gnome
the trapped ant prays
sometimes when it goes
really well, you wonder
"who's that at the piano?"
(cecil taylor) or
(from the blaskets)
even lard
has a right to its name

the placebo
send for the placebo

everyone did it

sometimes a fragment of language
illuminates a world not consistently round
breathing its air

Mechanical Gardens

what are the chances?
what do they want with the bowl?
morgan, eat your custard

Maltese Named Trouble

lone probe delivers no current
what is the sound who drive the life
decrease bycatch
dull, routine, poverty
facility for coldness
fairytales told adults
general betrayus

Viagra

does not function   a realistic fake that will disguise the fact that
wall where there was an elevated throne   made of you-know-
what on

not an easy one hoped jocular
me a few bruises.
joy!
crush her disguised growled other
blessedly brief. being surrounded by the military has always had a
why unhappily and tragically?
what we do now is put a little distance between us and those religious
closer latecomers hurried to their places. while we tuned up and

Pelf! Pelf!

in street and cold air
chromatophobia
wistful anger
form to formless
filters set to stun

broken biscuits
sack or save
so much depends
upon a myatonic
red-haired mucker

Thanks for the Memory

all that is alive merely evaporates
you don't want to remember

'small slices of pie
iraq or 9/11'

adamance was rewarded with
no one leaves this room, motherfucker

'all of the extraordinary records you set
in the area of drugs'

it was a chemical tuesday afternoon
clark was in petaluma

'reduce the uncertainty
that people confront'

investors retreated to safety
of government debt

Lippitude

what's the difference between f

ruled and governed?

metaphors for moods

talibanese

pink skirt in river

sad lonely memories of self

lost emotions

flat experience

to r or reduce or relate (it was politics)

erase or replace hidden memories

nothing but things
and cold perception

move hearing back and out

Reynard

memory of everything you do
except control

there shall be no other way
animal movements restart from midnight

thing wall
enough money out there

we eat lamb
musical cherapy

they hoped to find a job but failed
due to inexistent workforce demand

Icequakes

mister natural
sardines rice and treacle
frozen inca girl
twenty below

run roberts run
was it acton? noel road
joe orton joe meek
old kent road

at new cross
two a.m. cheapest
monopoly property
colin brian johnny

me in cold
orange haze
walking ten miles
to joe harriott

tubby hayes
rik gunnell
catlin's painting
shooting flamingos

my heart says
have a ball
mesothelioma
that girl from ilford

who could dance
in slush
fuck you
george bush

for Iain Sinclair

Rolled Homogeneous Armour

liquidation of inventory overhang
outward travel must not be in the past

below a new list
of potential ancestors

following catseyes of description
through darkness

birth
of expressed memory

burns institutionalised
fictions

Never Entered Mind

forgotten monkey amber
delights my introspection

but bubble massive armour
fermentation magnet arc

geek motherfucker instinct
fix mitochondria a

generous martini ice-cream
further messages arrive

germ mail illustrated
flashes medical alert

gone mental incandescence
flames melodically around

glitz mercury illicit
coagulability

Maul

all skeleton images are happy
hypocritical man of flesh
tree completes
recognised music laughter
where your horse is
every two minutes
with alert
quick or still
memory on abuse
dead interactive receivers
i don't forget
lisa
lake
your hairbrush sunlit
in amhurst road
carbon to diamond
graphite to pencil
utterly beautiful

Melody Road

a zipper hidden in the arm
city littered with brass

zipper hidden in the arm
a city littered with brass

poetry comes from maybe   bill viola

arsenal, ciao, gazette,
ghetto, gondola, lagoon,
lido, lazaret,
regatta, pantaloon

for Miles Champion

Data Death : Zerone

killing jews
it depends on how it's done
it depends on the circumstances
it depends on who does it

an invalid public movie atom
was found in the movie

Rivers of Bling

he entered wearing his beautiful white robe
highlights of which he had previously laid out for me
on the horizon for a while
old in unusual places

it was well-known that the shaykh enjoyed
a specific type of 'kraft' cheese
searching through a flash memory card
until that pale face emerged for real

for Jim Nisbet

Once and For All

creationists don't believe we evolve
not comforting we become the same
nobody will want that lucien
it's not a bit glamorous
and he just laughed

a tennis of texts to make
email irrelevant
oh dear says the pixel
i know now how ink felt

i seems
to remember
rotating ninja-bowl
rolls across flame
dated elements hold it back

Shuck

there is a series of moments
and this is one of them

our will is being tested,
but we are resolute

we have a better way
stay strong!

stay the course!
kill them!

be confident!
prevail!

we are going to wipe them out!
we are not blinking!

Seething with Adventure

modulated electricity wakes me
unusual attention

is a mirror
burnt polish

Chips

80 percent prefer chips to poetry

Birthday Poem

not into the etymology of gesture
watch death in your ear
reconcile god's teachings
with recreational shooting

and defence of self and country
driving around watering lawns
time will be vaporised
now of my three score years and ten

none will come again
canoe wife denies
pathetic lies
get the toll fee

rush of sentiment
down rail tracks
to igor, a green ground
who will i be then?

the pink is light
the yellow is bright
the red is the sun going down
the blue is the night

composer: stock music
is an occupation
listed under
other crew

with Florence Wylde Raworth

From Mountains and Gardens

privatised profits
socialised losses
illiquid buckets
toxic assets

jack sprat
jill downhill
bull under
bear mountain

sir violence
no penknives
dreams rough
adzed jelly

catchphrase graveyard
miss sister
randolf porter
von cholitz

one strand
who looks
back is
not i

orbitofrontal
cortex
my final
face

bodies
on the street
i can't
be everywhere

Capture of Karadzic

Kesostic
mAsostic
meRostic
mesAstic
mesoDtic
mesosZic
mesostIc
mesostiC

computer not a very handy tool
dulled thought too bored to record

that way
paving stone or badge

good soldier schweiss
world eyes'

revenge on
language

Never Odd or Even

seriously reading thoughts
made sense moving naturally
for several seconds barefoot
able to combine social situations
complete near light on glass
advantage carried their retreating forms
ski-ing in mind open but hidden

mask staring at time again
seriously reading thoughts
made sense moving naturally
carting one against line
for several seconds barefoot
advantage carried their retreating forms
ski-ing in mind open but hidden

vegetables still outsized ciphers
complete near light on glass
able to combine social situations
a gas station of chrome
envelope overpainted with glazes
mesh windows of incarceration
valuable in every pursuit

mask staring at time again
carting one against line
vegetables still outsized ciphers
envelope overpainted with glazes
valuable in every pursuit
mesh windows of incarceration
a gas station of chrome

looked at a thousand watts
peeled off a relaxed mass
metal room masked for painting
retreated to dry breath outside
smeared fury of her teeth
burned moment followed her hand
to canvas bent to look

looked at a thousand watts
smeared fury of her teeth
peeled off a relaxed mass
retreated to dry breath outside
metal room masked for painting
burned moments followed her hand
to canvas bent to look

History Portrayed by Lifesize Working Models

flip house
within boundaries of risk
tranche warfare
over the top

in the czech republic
trees contributed to
two hundred road deaths
last year

eat shit beef
or your produce
will be luxuries
for us

a tad more mercury
in your corn syrup?
reading paper money
in a furnace

Creaking Candle

false nose
a backheel
we try to please our guests
moonlight through quizzing-glass

our english jest
there is no extra charge for this extra charge

Over Noise

every second brought beauty
before vegetables before ancestors
thought grew thinner
everywhere except in pressed tales
thought that changed
regulated loose connections
losing slices of purity

characters crowded forests of masts
stamped skill with certainty
a bird joined dry bones
of puppet regimes off road
people remain afraid
within prisons of perception
without water

all dissipates into noise

Peanut Galleria

let loose the salmon, ella!
à la lanterne

thanks to hitler
allah put them in their place

said yusuf al qaradawi
another nut

Underground Mutton

in its very nature
relies on huge bogus content farms
using a diverse theme-based
set of content
usually generated in an automated fashion

or is that poetry?

I Wasn't Before

hand me the less lethal
to be good
what is seen
is learnt
nothing but that
but illusion

relief distorts

Looks Like We've Got Brain Matter

medium mogul
in missing seconds
flight tread mark
too old
how many
to not bother

?

Heat Up the Dead

around six a.m.
personality of blurred pixels
who did this to you
shaping objects
to obscure
internal possession

'marks'

Anti-Terrorism Started

running tap and plughole
almost comprehensible
certainly human
'if bored with water'
to be charged
for just obeying orders
not good career path
won't attract the
blastbeats that alternate
with nasty breaks
all day the scent ripe loquat
font: mirror on view
there is no work
there is disease
keep indoors
we have the outside covered
sucking last created need
not enough   good is better
please note this page
contains the name of god
if printed out please
treat it with appropriate respect
take an analgia
displayed system connected
to modification

All Knowledge

except in heads
electro magnetic pulse

electricity
magnetism

ignorance
between beeps

ribonucleotides
do it unwittingly.

emotions
may vary

wol holde
your shoulders

as you vomit
they find

their feet
you know the people

things have happened to them
you'll know later

put a pro-life bullet
in the doctor's head

i saw my skeleton
regard

Title Forgotten

where do they go
those things we know we know

brilliant blue g
walk with me

staring through print
into blind space of sound

fresh washed carrots
against blue shirt

unanticipated rightness
nothing wasted

Errata to *Collected Poems* (2003)

pp. xiv; xviii	catacoustics (1991)
p. 15	*they*
p. 17	that morning
p. 35	yes the sun i love *came* through
p. 83	'Sweep UP!' he
p. 87	This is MAINE
p. 100	why four lines and a stapler?
p. 115	you're in my light
p. 128	¡Qué Bonitos Ochos Tienes!
p. 130	¡que te vaya bien!
p. 159	among them
p. 184	a loupe
p. 214	so to speak
p. 248	capsules of air beneath the city: around them cartoon cats' eyes blink in the dark: above them molecules
p. 249	hung to dry.
p. 254	blurs our picture
p. 272	dinner's
p. 305	than a taste
pp. 312, 571	light in the first mood
p. 331	relámpago
pp. 386, 565	sentenced to death (title of sequence)
p. 438	still locked in combat
p. 488	sister in space (delete 'our')
p. 496	reasonably clearly mapped
p. 510	the necessity of ornament
p. 550	under sheet slowly (should align with line following)

My thanks to Matías Serra Bradford, Dave Cook, Nate Dorward, Gabriela Jauregui and Tony Lopez for close reading and sharp eyes.